Pray as You Can

A SHORT PRIMER

Mary Clare Vincent, OSB

FOREWORDS BY
*Esther de Waal and
M. Basil Pennington, OCSO*

PAULIST PRESS
New York / Mahwah, NJ

The Scripture quotations contained herein are from the New Revised Standard Version: Catholic Edition Copyright © 1989 and 1993, by the Division of Christian Education of the National Council of the Churches of Christ in the United States of America. Used by permission. All rights reserved.

Cover design by Sharyn Banks
Book design by Lynn Else

Copyright © 2011 by St. Scholastica Priory, Inc.

All rights reserved. No part of this book may be reproduced or transmitted in any form or by any means, electronic or mechanical, including photocopying, recording, or by any information storage and retrieval system without permission in writing from the Publisher.

Library of Congress Cataloging-in-Publication Data

Vincent, Mary Clare, 1925–
   Pray as you can : a short primer / Mary Clare Vincent ; forewords by Esther de Waal and M. Basil Pennington.
     p. cm.
   ISBN 978-0-8091-4734-2 (alk. paper)
   1. Prayer—Christianity. I. Title.
   BV213.V52 2011
   248.3'2—dc22

                                        2011008865

Published by Paulist Press
997 Macarthur Boulevard
Mahwah, New Jersey 07430

www.paulistpress.com

Printed and bound in the
United States of America

Contents

Foreword to the Paulist Press Edition
   by Esther de Waal v

Foreword to the Original Edition
   by Fr. M. Basil Pennington, OCSO vii

Introduction xi

Prologue xiii

1. Why Pray? 1

2. How Should I Pray? 7

3. When Should I Pray? 15

4. How Can I Pray Better? 21

5. How Do I Know I Am Advancing in Prayer? ...28

6. What About Distractions? 33

7. Am I Called to Contemplation? 37

8. Mary 46

To Rose and Sr. Margaret Catherine,
who know so well the way of prayer.

Foreword to the Paulist Press Edition

Some things in life remain constant, and among them prayer must surely be the most important for Christians. There are so many questions—How do I pray? Can I pray better? Should my prayer change? But above all, the insistent question that we must face at each new chapter of our lives—Why, why pray at all? The title that Sr. Mary Clare gave to her book when it first appeared in 1982 gives us the answer: Prayer is the way to God.

That is why the writing of books on prayer will never cease. Each new voice brings its own emphasis, a unique emphasis, a particular approach. We can each of us point to books that spoke to us at the right time. But we also find ourselves coming back to writing that is clear and profound, and so can we read and reread, and share it with others.

That is why I was delighted when out of the blue came a letter from Sr. Mary Clare, with a copy of her book, and a request that I write a short foreword. There was no hesitation. The postman dropped the package onto my kitchen table, and I sat there enthralled, with the sound of the waterfall outside, and the line of the Welsh hillside beyond, and was carried back to my many happy visits to Petersham and the sharing of talk, community, and prayer.

I think that it was John Main who said that we must recognize that prayer means "seeking to live our lives on the bedrock of reality." Here this essential truth is presented to us again. The title says it all: Prayer is the way to God.

Esther de Waal
Feast of the Epiphany, 2009

Foreword to the Original Edition

The appearance in the West of many Swamis and Rochis from the ancient religions of Asia has been a frightening thing for many Christians. But I have rather seen and experienced it as an invigorating challenge and a recall to some of the neglected values of our own tradition, which has its own antiquity and richness. Not the least of these values is the role of the spiritual teacher, the master, who shares the ministry of the Lord in calling forth his disciples to a fuller, richer living out of his transcendent yet very human-fulfilling teachings. Happily in our Christian tradition this life-engendering role has never been restricted to the male. Through all the centuries we look to great spiritual mothers, from Macrina and Paula to those two Doctors of the Church, Catherine of Siena and Teresa of Avila.

I had to smile when I received Mother Mary Clare's manuscript with the gentle request for a foreword. At that very moment, I was in the process of writing a very similar book for another publisher—even some of the chapter headings were the same. As I read Mother's manuscript, I rejoiced. The teaching is very much the same, but the approach very different. I appreciated again the richness of our tradition and the enriching complementarity of the sexes. Mother Mary Clare writes with the sure hand of a well-experienced spiritual mother.

Simple, straight, clear teaching on prayer is what is sought today as it was in the early days of the church. And it is found here. Take for example the crispness of this question and answer: "How do you know God is acting? The very fact that such a question is asked proves this state is from God. Lukewarm, mediocre souls have no anxiety about serving him." And this: "The desire for prayer is prayer, the prayer of desire." And finally, to cite just one more gem: "Let us always bear in mind that we are praying, not because we love prayer, but because we love God."

There is a simplicity and sharpness in Mother's teaching. There is also depth and beauty; an insight that will resonate with what is deepest in us as human beings and Christians.

Mother's simple, rich teaching is not her own. It is drawn from the exceedingly rich teaching of the Christian tradition. Mother bejewels her text with many quotations, not only from the divinely inspired Scriptures but also from a wonderful array of fellow Christians who have meditated upon the sacred texts and shared their experience of faith: Saint Irenaeus and Father van Zeller, Saint Augustine and Charles Péguy, Blessed John Ruysbroeck and Padre Pio, and many others. The selection is rich and always appropriate.

In a special way did I rejoice in the chapter on the Blessed Virgin Mary.

Read and be delighted even as you are nourished and guided.

Fr. M. Basil Pennington, OCSO
Feast of St. Teresa of Avila, 1981

Introduction

This little book on the life of prayer and the way to God started as a series of meditative conferences given to a group of men and women who, having found them helpful in their own lives of prayer, urged me to gather them together into chapters and publish them in order to reach a wider audience. The style is necessarily informal, colloquial, and practical, and not at all scientific or scholarly. Since there are many methods of prayer and many ways to God, no attempt has been made to cover them all or even to refer to them all. If the few suggestions I offer here help but one person, my efforts will not have been wasted.

Prologue

In the cruel, unsettling years of the Roman Empire from AD 250 to AD 313, when Christianity was regarded as synonymous with treason, the deserts of Palestine, Syria, and North Africa began to overflow with a strange brand of refugees known as anchorites or hermits. These Christians seemed at first to be fleeing from their pagan persecutors or from a pagan environment; but when, in 313, religious tolerance was granted to them and migration to the desert redoubled, it was obvious that the mysterious immigrants were not so much running away from something bad, as running after something very good. They were in fact seeking the life of prayer and the way to God.

They lived in separate huts, caves, abandoned tombs, and deserted temples, each one seeking his own uncharted way to God but coming together every Sunday in church for the synaxis (gathering) and breaking of the bread and spiritual instruction. *For they believed that life without prayer, asceticism, and guidance was worthless.* These hermits hardly ever ate or slept or spoke. They prayed and sang psalms; they wove baskets and mats that they sold or bartered for their scanty needs and gave the surplus to the poor. The desert dwellers were humble and silent folk, preferring solitude and obscurity to sociality and prestige. Despite their reluctance, crowds of disciples speedily gathered around them so that by the end of the fourth century, some one hundred thousand solitaries of both sexes had found their way into the desert and their numbers began to equal the population of the towns. (Oxyrhynchus, one of their silent encampments, had ten thousand monks and twenty thousand nuns all bent on the quest for God and their own true selves with ascetic endeavor, in the spirit of the Gospel: "he who loses his life for my sake will find it."

Many of the things the desert folk said to their disciples have come down to us and they are as relevant in our desperate modern world as they were in the desperate ancient world. The experienced ones, having explored the frontiers of human nature in its encounter with God, instructed the inexperienced and gave concrete remedies that they themselves had practiced and found to work. *The less you pray, they warned, the worse for you!* The life of prayer is indeed the way to God.

What do the desert fathers and mothers have to say to men and women today? To begin with, the questions they were asked by their disciples are the same that are asked by men and women today: Why pray? How should I pray? When should I pray? How can I pray better? How do I know if I am praying well? What about distractions? Am I called to contemplation?

CHAPTER 1
Why Pray?

> One of the old men of the desert said: Pray attentively and soon you will straighten out your life and your thoughts.

A life without prayer doesn't work. The need to pray, linked as it is to our longing for love and understanding, self-knowledge, and happiness, has been put in us by God and it is meant to be fulfilled. It is the most human of operations, as necessary and nourishing as eating, and the most divine. It is transcending to our souls, lifting our innermost reality to the supernatural realm of faith. It discloses our hearts to God and in him somehow we discover ourselves. The desert dwellers found themselves, their true selves, in Christ. They were free. We too have known free people whose lives are filled with God. They have an inner peace and harmony no matter what their outer circumstances are. We have all met such peace-filled persons, loving God, living a life of charity, quietly heroic, and unnoticed by the world: a self-sacrificing, hard-working mother, a pure-hearted, generous man, a dedicated, responsible son or daughter—people who make a space in their lives for God; like the very successful businessman, free of tension, who recently admitted that he spent half his lunch hour in reading or meditating on the scriptures, and a half hour of work time in reading spiritual books or thinking over quietly what he had read.

We are meant to create deep within ourselves an inner order so that we can look upon God within us; otherwise our spirit will die and we'll find ourselves in the predicament described by St. Paul in his first letter to the Corinthians (3:17):

> *If anyone destroys God's temple, God will destroy that person. For God's temple is holy, and* you *are that temple.*

The temple of God is built up by prayer, for there is a self-healing mechanism within us that is activated by prayer. But sometimes that which heals us is what we would run away from. If we put ourselves in God's hands, can we go wrong? Won't he take care of us? People who pray will answer yes. They go to God with their afflictions, fears, frustrations, sorrows and betrayals. Slowly he reveals himself to them and transforms their lives. "Come to me, all you that are weary and are carrying heavy burdens, and I will give you rest" (Matt 11:28). Only in God will we find peace. The burdens may remain but we find their meaning and place in our lives; our values change and our souls are refreshed.

I was vividly reminded of this not long ago at a workshop on contemplative and centering prayer. During one of the discussions, a widow shared with us her feelings when she learned that her eighteen-year-old unwed daughter was pregnant—a situation prevalent enough today. Her first reaction was resentment, grief, shame, and anger—anger against her daughter, anger against God. She felt put upon by the Lord and betrayed by her daughter. In the midst of her anguish she prayed and after a while she found an unexplainable strength, so that she was able to speak calmly to her daughter: "I want you to know I love you unconditionally. I'm not going to say I'm not hurt or humiliated or approving the action that brought about your pregnancy. But you're my child and I love you." Further prayer brought the widow to a new level of consciousness, enabling her to see within *herself* dark areas of pride, possessiveness, false values, and a spirit exhausted by sin. She saw the redemptive power of repentance and love, God triumphing in the midst of sin, and loving her unconditionally as she loved her daughter. Because of the daughter's humiliation, the family was drawn together, their love for one another increased, their faith was revitalized and assumed a wholly new and higher dimension.

After the infant's birth the daughter said, "Mother, your faith carried me through. Now because of it, I have faith myself." Experience indeed bears out that God is constantly inviting us to participate in his own fructifying love.

When we turn to God in prayer, we turn to one who is already within us and waiting. "The soul does not have to ask God to listen," explains Hubert van Zeller; "God has been listening before it entered into the head of the soul to ask—search we must but always we should know that our search is not the cause of his presence. Our search is merely one of the effects" (*The Holy Rule: Notes on St. Benedict's Legislation for Monks* [London: Sheed and Ward], 1958). The word of God is truly the light that enlightens every man that comes into the world and of his fullness we have *all* received. And the astonishing truth is not man's search for God, but God's search for man. "There is one God the Father," says St. Irenaeus, "and one Christ Jesus our Lord, who comes by a universal dispensation and recapitulates all things in himself. But in 'all things' man also is comprised, a creature of God; therefore, he recapitulates man in himself" (*Against the Heresies*, 3.16.3).

God, then, created man; man sins; God does not abandon him but recovers him and draws him back into his own divine life. While man has a spontaneous, unreflecting hunger for God and is constantly in search of him in whose image he is made, God also, spontaneous but free, is even more in search of man whose spirit was created precisely so that it can reach the perfection of image that is already in him. For God is the bird that searches for the hunter, the fountain that pants for the deer, the bread that hungers for the hungry. *Sitivit sitiri Deus*, says St. Augustine. *God thirsts to be thirsted after*. He has loved us into being, into repentance, into fullness of divine life. He asks only for our surrender in prayer—for *our* sakes. "Before you call upon me, I will say to you, 'Behold, here I am.'" In finding God or rather in letting him find us, we participate once more in his riches, in his eternal life, given to us in grace and made present to us here and now. "Grace is shrewd and unexpected," writes Charles Péguy. "And it is stubborn—when one throws it out the door, it comes in again by the window—when it's not coming straight, it's coming sideways." This is the gift of God—and our dignity lies in our need for him!

"We have too many men of science, too few men of God," declared General Omar Bradley some years ago. "We have grasped the mystery of the atom and rejected the sermon on the mount....we know more about war than we know about peace, more about killing than we know about living." The cybernetic age with all its advantages and achievements cannot possibly satisfy our spiritual longings or solve our inward problems, or see us through life's deep nervous exhaustion of listening to the noisy conveniences surrounding us or the burden of acquiring and maintaining them! The gospels admonish us not to lay up for ourselves treasures on earth where rust and moth consume and thieves break in and steal, but lay up for ourselves treasures in heaven where neither rust nor moth consume nor thieves break in and steal; for where our treasure is there also will our heart be (Matt 6:19–21).

We have been made to the image and likeness of God, which means we are capable of living the divine life. Not only capable, we are *meant* to live the divine life. And so, to go against God, to abandon him, is to go against nature and to abandon our very selves. "You have made us for yourself, O Lord," cries St. Augustine, "and our heart is restless until it rests in you." Prayer is the means whereby we find our rest in God and come to that divine oneness of action and will for which we yearn and which will lead us into eternal life for which we were created. And if at times the way of prayer is arduous and uphill, we should recall the Chinese saying that the journey of a thousand miles begins with a single step. Therefore, "walk while you have the light," says the Lord. "Follow me: I am the Way"; and "Peace be with you!"

CHAPTER 2
How Should I Pray?

The Abbot Isaac said: "There are as many kinds of prayers as there are conditions and characters of souls.…For each one prays in one way when he is happy, in another when he is sad, in another when he is lifted up by spiritual achievements, in another when he is cast down by attacks, in another when he is asking pardon for his sins, in another when he is asking for some grace or virtue, in another when he is in danger, in another when he is in peace and security, in another when he is enlightened by the revelation of heavenly mysteries, and in another when he is discouraged by a sense of weakness in virtues and dryness in feeling. And so the Apostle says: 'I exhort therefore first of all that supplication, prayers, intercessions, thanksgivings be made' (1 Tim 2:3)."

Too often we think of prayer as a sheerly human activity, a monologue we direct to God. We forget that prayer is a gift, a grace, something God does in us. It is an umbrella term that has many ramifications. As one old man of the desert, using the Bible as a basis, said: "The Canaanite woman cries out and she is heard

(Matt 15); the woman with the issue of blood is silent and she is called blessed (Luke 8); the Pharisee uses many words and he is condemned (Matt 9); the publican does not dare open his mouth and he is heard (Luke 18)."

We must approach God with a humble attitude of listening, waiting, asking: "Lord, teach us to pray." We must saturate our souls with scripture, with the beauty of the mysteries of faith, under the inspiration of the Spirit of God who alone teaches us how we should pray (Rom 8:26). For Christian prayer is never the prayer of an individual—it is linked to the Trinity and to the church.

Even when I pray alone, it is the prayer of the community, the people of God, of the Body of Christ, the church that is Christ. My prayer is thus identified with the prayer of Christ. Our sufferings, our crosses, our daily living must be permeated with this spirituality. It is an experience of death, this giving up of our individuality, but it is also an experience of rising, and we find fulfillment only in losing ourselves in Christ. "[Y]our life is hidden with Christ in God" (Col 3:3). Meister Eckhart, the Rhineland mystic, wrote: "If a man would completely yield himself but for a moment, all things would be given him—Were I to go wholly outside myself and empty myself entirely—oh! the Father from Heaven would beget His only begotten Son in my spirit so purely that the Spirit would again beget Him." And St. Nicholas of Flue used to pray: "Take away, Lord, everything that keeps me from you." This is St. Paul's *kenosis* (emptying). Or as St. Bonaventure puts it: "Love always follows deprivation."

Four broad patterns of prayer in the desert tradition are: (1) *lectio divina* (prayerful reading); (2) *meditation* (using the mind and imagination in reflection on what one has read); (3) *oratio* (petitions, thanksgiving, praise); (4) *contemplation* (awareness of God without the need of many words or thoughts). We should not choose among these four aspects but alternate them, letting one flow in and out of the other, letting one so influence the other that our prayer life is a unified whole rather than a series of fragmented practices. Since God speaks in and through many ways, we should respond accordingly. "Seek in reading and you shall find in meditation. Knock in *oratio* and it shall be opened to you in contemplation"—this was the only method of prayer the ancients knew. Undergirding it all was the need to know and love God.

Moderns systematize prayer and fragmentize it as discursive prayer, affective prayer, meditation, and contemplation, each as distinct or progressive phases. The ancients had no such distinctions. They sang psalms and paused after each one to ruminate on what they had sung. They memorized scripture and during their work, they silenced the banalities of the mind by repeating what they had memorized. In the middle of *lectio divina* they made acts of love. They didn't confine or concern themselves with the right method or the mechanics of prayer. They let the Spirit pray within them. "Our age is particularly given to introspection and the analysis of motive and action," warns Karl Rahner, "with the result that we are often deprived of the power to act through sheer preoccupation with how the act is to be done." One kind of prayer should flow freely back and forth from the other. Dialogical reading and meditation, thanksgiving, petition, praise, contemplation, wonder at God's bounty, respect for his creation, loving attention to his beauty—these were the planks in the ancients' platform of prayer.

We should not stop our reading or meditation or praise and petition, or efforts to develop our contemplation unless God intervenes and, as St. Teresa of Avila says, "suspends the understanding and makes it cease from its acts, and puts before it what astonishes and occupies it so that without making any reflection it can understand and comprehend what we could only understand in years with all the effort in the world."

Prayer is a matter of love, and so scripture makes sense when it exhorts *Pray always*. This injunction springs from the first commandment: You shall love the Lord your God with your whole heart and your whole mind and your whole soul and your whole strength. When you love someone deeply, your love is continual, manifesting itself in diverse ways. Above all, you don't worry over what you'll talk about when you meet. It's only of strangers that you say, "What will I talk about with that person?" God is no stranger. He is our Father, our redeemer, our sanctifier, more interior to us than we are to ourselves. Jesus said, "I have not called you servants but friends." And when he was asked specifically by his disciples how to pray, he answered, "When you pray, say Our Father. Acknowledge your weakness and dependence on God. And don't use many words. Be simple, like children. The Father knows beforehand what you need."

If prayer is a conversation, how can you methodize it? We must become very little with the Lord if he is to do great things in us, because he regards the lowliness of his handmaid. Prayer is a raising of the heart and mind to God. It's accepting the fact that God loves us. (To be loved is an astonishing thing. It is also an invitation to receive.) Prayer is a conversation with God—which means we must be silent, too, and listen. It is a spiritual attitude, a way of resting with and in God.

A retreat master I know once said, "Prayer is accepting pain; prayer is rest; it is sorrow, it is touching God and friends with loving hands. Prayer is a silence of the heart, a welcome to God's creation and all God's people. Prayer is God-made-flesh; it is ministry to the sick, the poor, and the lonely. It is not necessarily prayer when we are alone and neither is it not prayer when we are not alone. To pray means also to change."

Scripture tells us our prayer should be simple. "Seek him in simplicity of heart" (Wis 1:1, NJB). And so the desert fathers often advised short acts of prayer, ejaculations drawn from scripture. A favorite phrase was "O God, come to my help," or the Jesus Prayer formula, "Jesus, son of David, have mercy on me." Simple acts of faith (my God, I believe you are within me); of hope (I hope for your mercy); of love (my God, I love you) or short, spontaneous phrases of our own arising out of the heart—these were excellent practices they advised.

When the Abbot Macarius was asked by one of the brethren how he should pray, he answered: "There is no need to use many words. Only stretch out your arms and say: Lord, have pity on me as you will and as you know how! And if the enemy persecutes you, say: 'Lord, come to my help!' " As Dom John Chapman puts it, it is useful to repeat certain words or short phrases to keep the imagination quiet—like throwing a bone to a dog to keep him quiet while he gnaws on it. (It also prepares the soul for contemplation.) "Pray as you can," he used to exhort, "not as you can't," which is a new twist to St. Augustine's phrase: "Love and do what you will."

One preliminary warning on the ways of prayer: we must expect to go through the night of the senses and the night of the spirit. There is an active and a passive dimension to both. The active is what *we* do, the passive is what *God* does to us.

The active night of the senses lies in the penances we impose on ourselves, for example. The passive night of the senses consists of sufferings God sends us.

In the active night of the spirit, we mortify our will and intellect. There can be no deep prayer without mortification and discipline: exterior done primarily by ourselves, interior done primarily by God. We are weak; we love to enjoy our own sanctity—the surest way of losing it. Trials purify us and God proportions them to our need to be emptied of self. "God is faithful, and he will not let you be tested beyond your strength, but with the testing he will also provide the way out so that you may be able to endure it" (1 Cor 10:13).

The Lord knows we need to struggle in order to grow. Nature bears this out too. In this connection, I remember reading about a fisherman who, in between fishing trips, used to store the fish he caught in tanks so that they might be fresh when he returned. He noticed, however, that the fish in the tanks never were as savory as the ones freshly caught until he thought of adding catfish to the tanks. Though a few fish perished, the survivors tasted better for having fought and struggled against their enemy. "It is good that at times we are called upon to bear adversities and crosses," we read in the *Imitation of Christ*, "for these oftentimes induce a man to reenter his own heart."

If at times we seem to be losing our way, losing our time, and losing our senses, we must go on in faith, content never to be content. God has a way of leading us into the desert just when we think all is well—like the Israelites who after marching safely through the Red Sea with Moses were led immediately into the desert where the Lord put them to the test. So we must continue steadfast in the life of prayer, never really knowing how much we have progressed, or rather, knowing that no matter how far we go, we are beginners all our life until the end when God shall appear and "then we shall be like him for we shall see him as he is."

CHAPTER 3
When Should I Pray?

A certain old man of the desert was passing by the cell of a young monk whom he saw restlessly working in a building and repairing what was unnecessary. From a distance he watched the young brother breaking a stone with a heavy hammer, and he noticed also a devil standing over the brother—though unseen by him—and together with him striking the blows and urging him on. Whenever the brother wanted to stop, the demon urged him to continue. The old man, disgusted at the illusion, approached the young man and asked, "Why are you working so hard?" "We have to," replied the young man wearily. "Well do you say 'we,'" answered the Elder, "for you are not alone." And he explained to the younger man the temptation of the Evil One and how he must establish his soul in peace by freeing himself from the compulsion of overwork.

Most people do not have to be convinced of the necessity of prayer, but the problems we encounter in our efforts to pray are many and discouraging as we live our rushed and feverish lives. We have a home and family to take care of, a job to work at, parties to give and go to, business meetings to attend, appointments of all kinds, family matters to settle. How can we find time to pray? But how do we find time to do these other things? And why do we always say, "I'm too busy to pray," and not, "I'm too busy to work"? Work, as we all know, fills up the time we give it. Sometimes work is a way of escaping the loneliness we feel within. What is especially tragic about the condition of modern man and what heightens his emptiness and isolation is an incessant preoccupation with external activity and a lack of communication with God. If we direct our minds toward God as the source, the center, and the totality of our lives, we will spontaneously start moving on to a higher level of life, and we will find ourselves doing less but accomplishing more. Our goals will expand, our desire for a simpler life will grow, our interior senses will be sharpened, our self-knowledge will increase, love will be an accompanying element in our work, and as love for God grows, love for others will become our main concern. The few moments of solitude we may have to steal from a busy day will be inspired by love: love of God and love of man; and our solitude, far from separating us from those we love, will be the space wherein we find them.

This experience is illustrated by someone I know, a mother of five young children, who gets up a half hour before the rest of her family—the only time her house is quiet—to practice centering (contemplative) prayer. Although most of her prayer experience is dry, once in a rare while she is so caught up in the knowledge that God loves her, she needs no more security to carry on, and the effects last for months. It is noticeable to all that each person, child or adult, she encounters is the object of her total attention and care. Her daily living is permeated with the divine energy.

The Bible makes clear the place that prayer should occupy in our lives. "Let nothing stop you from praying always," we read in the Old Testament (Sir 18:22, Douay-Rheims). "Pray without ceasing, give thanks in all circumstances; for this is the will of God," exhorts St. Paul (1 Thess 5:17–18). "Pray always and do not lose heart," cautions Our Lord (Luke 18:1). "We have not been commanded to work unceasingly or to watch and fast unceasingly," shrewdly observes Evagrius, a fourth-century monk of Pontus, "but the law requires us in the words of the Apostle to pray unceasingly."

Now we know the Bible does not command the impossible nor does Christ ask us to do anything he didn't do himself. He forgave his enemies, he healed his persecutors, he visited the sick, he fed the hungry, he consoled the sorrowful, he *prayed without ceasing*. We can learn from this that to pray without ceasing doesn't mean always to be isolated from people and from our work. It means living for and loving God entirely. It means letting him take over in our lives, opening ourselves to his love, judging the absolute value of anything or of any work from his point of view.

"Whether you eat or drink or do anything else," says St. Paul, "do all for the glory of God." We pray when we are trying to be what God wants us to be (our true selves); to do what God wants us to do; to want to be what God wants us to be and to want to do what God wants us to do. We pray to God by cooking—if that is what we should be doing—by washing the dishes, mowing the lawn, by talking kindly to our neighbor, and finally by stopping all noise, and raising our mind and heart to God in contemplation. The hardest thing is to know when to do one and when the other, when to cook or wash the dishes, when to mow the lawn, when to speak to our neighbor, and when to leave space to contemplate. There are some who can cook and wash and mow and speak without interrupting their contemplation. God has given us a conscience to guide us, and if we are humble, the Holy Spirit will help us, and speak to us within and without and through others.

> A young man asked a desert father what good work he should do so as to have eternal life. The old man answered: "Not all works are equal. For scripture says that Abraham was hospitable and God was with him. And David was humble and God was with him. And Elias loved the solitary prayer and God was with him. So, do whatever you see your soul desires according to God and guard your heart."

Love is the indispensable element.

The saints tell us that the demons strive day and night to prevent us from praying—by turning our minds from the Lord, by temptations of one kind or another. St. Albert claims that the devil envies man's life of prayer: "He is always trying to turn man's mind away from his Lord God, now by one temptation or passion, now by another. At one time he fills him with unnecessary care and indiscreet anxiety; at another he casts him among crowds and makes him spend himself in dissolute conversation and senseless curiosity. Then again he beguiles him by the study of subtle books, by irrelevant talk, by rumor and news; or he assails him with hardships and besets him with hostilities."

Sometimes *we* are the demon, filling our lives with trivia so we can't hear God. "Cast off dead works," admonishes St. Gregory Nazianzen, "and give place to the spirit." We must create within ourselves an inner order. We can't be attentive ordinarily to God if there is continual clatter in our lives, just as the more one talks, the less one listens. (Someone has noticed that *listen* and *silent* have the same letters.) Those who love listen for God's voice, and they hear him speak in their hearts, a "conversation in silence."

"To pray," St. Alphonsus assures us, "it is not necessary always to be kneeling or in church or even in some quiet corner at home, though it is advisable when possible to adopt a reverent attitude in some place where you are not exposed to distractions. You can pray while you work, you can pray while walking down the street, in any place, under all circumstances, by raising your mind to God and thinking of the passion of Christ, or any other pious subject."

Since prayer should not be separated from daily living, it *is* possible to pray always, for to pray is to love. Just as husband and wife love each other by their fidelity, sacrificing and working for and with each other, so too we pray when we are intent on doing what God wants us to do. To know what he wants us to do, we must simply turn to him and ask. Then quiet down and listen. "Ask, and it will be given you; search, and you will find; knock, and the door will be opened for you" (Matt 7:7–8). If you don't have time to ask or seek and knock, *steal* the time. Leave the clutter of your lives and let go—in God!

CHAPTER 4
How Can I Pray Better?

> The Abbot Nilus said: "If you want to pray properly, do not let yourself be upset or you will run in vain." And he added, "Do not always want things to turn out as you think it should but as God wills, then you will be peaceful and thankful in your prayer."

All our lives we have to ask humbly, "Lord, teach us to pray." Then we will come to realize that the more we know the more there is to know—that prayer is many things: It is loving more than thinking, a receiving more than an achieving, a laying aside of our thoughts, an admission that God is greater than our ideas of him. It is a treasure hidden in a field, which we get only by junking everything we have; it is a reaching out beyond ourselves to find God, and it is also an entering into ourselves to find him within.

God has appointed a time for everything and for every business under the heavens (Eccl 3:11). He has made everything proper to its time. There is a time for prayerful reading and a time for meditation; a time for petition and praise; a time for contemplation and silence. We have to make an effort to know when to do one and when to do the other while recognizing it all as a gift from God, for Christian prayer is a matter of grace. It flows out of and back into our daily living, a continual dying and rising, a repeated beginning. We must learn to stay in touch with the Spirit, to discover which path to follow in our approach to the center of our lives wherein we find God.

If sacred reading reminds us of the presence of God (for twenty years St. Teresa of Avila knew no other way), we should stay with it until we find our own reflections or vocal expressions more useful. When these tire us, we should seek God in contemplation, a type of prayer and of experience, which is the fullness of love and unifies our whole being in God. The cycle of prayer is completed by contemplation not as a thing imposed from without, but as the prime mover and cause from the beginning and the crown and consummation of all our being and activity.

Christian contemplation quickly shows us that we can't be neutral about ourselves, our neighbor, or God. We have to know what and who we are, what and who is my neighbor, and what and who is God. The knowledge is necessary but crushing for we can't know all that we are, nor are we, or our neighbor, or God exactly what we know of them. No matter how desperately we want to know ourselves, the mystery of self and the mystery of our greatnesses and weaknesses will never be fully unraveled in this life. There are unknown deserts within us, obscure depths we dare not even explore yet are subject to, as long as we are not at least aware of them. Indeed awareness of these Saharas of our hearts would destroy and devastate us were we to tackle them alone, without the light of faith. God alone can show us "the mystery of iniquity" because he alone is within us, sustaining us in being, loving us while we are sinners, reconciling us to himself by the death of his son. The power to harmonize the discordances within us comes from the soul giving itself over to the divine action. "Live by the Spirit," cries St. Paul, "and do not gratify the desires of the flesh. For what the flesh desires is opposed to the Spirit, and what the Spirit desires is opposed to the flesh; for these are opposed to each other, to prevent you from doing what you want" (Gal 5:16–17).

We must learn to stay in touch with the Spirit to discover which path to follow in our approach to the center of our life wherein we find God. It isn't always easy. There are definite indications given to guide us, however, and St. John of the Cross, with other masters of the spiritual life, gives three main signs that show that God is leading the soul to another kind of prayer:

1. It becomes more and more difficult to meditate or use the mind and imagination. Where before it was easy to read prayerfully and then consider in detail some incident from the Bible, the day (or rather, night) comes when all sensible joy, interest, and fervor dry

up. The anguished soul is bereft of consolation; it is bone dry and bored.

2. Unable to meditate, the soul has no desire for piety of any kind, or penance, or good works. Sadness, depression, distaste for the spiritual set in. Yet—and this is important—there is no desire for created things. The things of the world are just as boring as the things of God.

3. The soul has a great longing for God. It is worried and anxious that because of infidelity it has lost him. The spiritual life seems to be disappearing and grace gone. If all three signs are present, in varying degrees of intensity, they should be regarded not only as trials but as very great, positive graces. They are necessary if the soul is to advance. God is treating the soul as a mother treats her baby. When the baby is newborn the mother "warms it in her bosom, nourishes it with her milk, feeds it with tender and delicate food, carries it in her arms and fondles it. But as the child grows older, the mother withholds her caresses, hides her breasts and anoints them with bitter aloes. She won't carry the baby in her arms anymore but makes it walk on the ground, so that losing the habits of a baby, it may apply itself to greater and more substantial pursuits" (*Dark Night*, book 1, ch. 1, n. 2). God himself then has put the soul into a state of dryness in order to free it from the slavery to the senses.

How do you know it is God acting? Perhaps it is one's own fault and infidelity? The very fact that such a question is asked proves this state is from God. Lukewarm, mediocre souls have no anxiety about serving him.

These are the darknesses we must go through in order to profit from our spiritual reading, our meditation, and our prayer. These are the nights the contemplative must go through before he or she sees the dawn. The first is a long dryness when spiritual things lose their attractiveness; the second comes when meditation is no longer possible. The soul is exhausted, like a worn out athlete, exhausted, and yet running aimlessly back and forth. The imagination is insensible to the things of God and wide open to all other impressions. This is the passage from meditation to a simpler prayer. The last night is the worst of all. But the blacker the night, the greater the purification and the deeper the union with God. Not the least of trials here is believing you are wasting your time at prayer and that you are betraying God, yourself, and your neighbor.

St. Benedict advises us when faced with trials "to embrace patience with a quiet conscience, and not grow weary or give in, as the scripture says: 'He that shall persevere to the end shall be saved,' (Matt 10:22) and again, 'Let your heart be comforted and wait for the Lord' (Ps 26:14)" (RB 35–37). "Proper to prayer also is this humble and confident attitude throughout the night when not even a glimmer of the coming dawn is any longer perceived. The night of obedience in the fourth degree of humility is the Benedictine parallel to the nights described in the tradition of St. John of the Cross," adds André Louf. "The two traditions are mutually dependent and the one should help to illumine the other."

Let us remember, too, that Christ is with us and part of us when we are suffering. "I am the vine, you are the branches," he says, implying that all men are born in him (note Tertullian, in the third century, declaring that man by nature is Christian, *naturaliter Christianus*). If we do not respond, we are cut off. If we do respond, we are pruned. So suffering is the destiny of everyone. But the vine also suffers. Christ, therefore, suffers when anyone rejects him; he also suffers in the just, that they may bear fruit. Indeed, in them, his suffering is prolonged for the pruning is repeated.

Our hope should be that God will work within us, pruning us and expanding our hearts as the psalm says: "Lord, expand my soul." We will see better and better in the darkness especially as we get used to it. It is a darkness full of peace and light, for even though we are walking in the dark valley, we need fear no evil for God is with us; his rod and his staff will comfort us. Let us pray, then, as God wants us to pray, never entirely giving up reading, meditation, or vocal prayers. Let us be satisfied with God's way of leading us like men and women who wait patiently for their Lord. St. Ignatius reminds us, "Few suspect what God would do in their souls if only they would let him do it!" The work is his; our main job is to get out of the way.

When we are tempted to discouragement because of darkness, dryness, or anxiety, let us remember the prayer of Jesus in the garden. His soul was "sorrowful unto death." He was alone; he felt the bitterness of the "chalice" he was to drink. Yet his perseverance in the prayer of acceptance in the midst of struggle (*agonia*) gave him that peace that astounds all who contemplate his death on the cross.

CHAPTER 5
How Do I Know I Am Advancing in Prayer?

> One of the old men of the desert used to say: As a bee, wherever he goes, makes honey, so anyone who is doing the will of God will always produce the spiritual sweetness of good works.

How can we know our prayer is pleasing to God? By its effects and by its fruits. The results are very obvious and very definite, for whatever God touches, he floods with the riches of his being—he is so great that the mere thought of him can elevate a man. He has given us a model. That model is Christ, and our destiny is to be changed entirely into Christ. Authentic prayer effects that change. It can be achieved if we cooperate with the Father, for we are called by the Father to this destiny. We are called to live the life of the Holy Spirit in the Son. The Spirit leads us to the paschal mystery that Christ lived in the world, and since the Holy Spirit is in our subconscious (or "supraconscious," to quote Maritain), we are not aware of him, yet we are full of light for he leads us to light—*through darkness*. Our destiny will be fulfilled if we remember our model—Christ. St. Paul refers to Christ as "the yes." In him there is no "yes" and "no," he says, but there is only "yes." Christ is the yes to the Father. We must imitate the personality and reality of the Son who is yes to the Father, yes in perfect obedience to the Father.

"Learn of me," says the Son, "for I am meek and humble of heart." The more authentic our prayer—which is, according to the desert tradition, a communion with God—the more we see our littleness and nothingness. Fortunately, there is another polarity in our experience that faith supplies: the certainty—dark and obscure at times—of the strength that is God's. As St. Teresa of Avila, having only two ducats (about two dollars) to her name and faced with building a convent, wittily and wisely observed: "Teresa and two ducats are nothing, but *God*, Teresa and two ducats are everything." Then she proceeded to set up convents all over Spain. This teaches that prayer helps us to keep two concepts in mind: the weakness that is mine and the strength that is God's. In confessing our weakness, we draw down God's strength. The weaker we confess we are, the more God helps us. St. Paul exults: "I will boast all the more gladly of my weaknesses, so that the power of Christ may dwell in me" (2 Cor 12:9). "Come to me you who are burdened," promises Christ, "and I will refresh you." We should realize that we can get nowhere without the grace of God—"without me, you can do nothing," says Christ. The better our prayer life, the more literally do we accept this.

When we turn to ourselves, we will see all our own failings and shortcomings; when we turn to our neighbor, we will see only his or her needs. When we turn to God, we will see only his loving strength. Prayer effects this transformation. Blessed John Ruysbroeck says of the interior man, "He dwells in God and yet goes forth toward all creatures in universal love, in virtues, and in justice." Prayer thus sublimates and spiritualizes every part of our life; it is the most effective means of progress in virtue. As St. Pio of Pietrelcina puts it, "It is the best weapon we possess, the key that opens the heart of God." Our love for God and our love for others become our main concern. We become, through prayer, concerned with our brother's need. Above all with his greatest need—the need for love. We learn to give him our time, our talents, our trust, our concern, and awareness of his needs. St. John posits the startling principle that as Christ laid down his life, we ought to lay down our lives for the brethren. This is the basis of the Gospel ethic. According to Navalis: "He who once seeks God, ends by finding him everywhere." We can add, especially is he found in our neighbor. We never go to God and leave people behind or out of it. The most cloistered monks and nuns, far from deserting their neighbor, show their love and deep concern for others by their prayers for them. Their solitude is an expansion, an intensification of their membership in the Body of Christ. They truly witness to St. Jerome's statement: "Never less alone than when alone." They are the world's representatives before God, like Moses who asked the Lord to pardon and not to punish the Israelites for their rebellion and the Lord answered: "I do forgive, just as you have asked" (Num 14:20).

Though prayer is possible at all times and under all circumstances, some solitude and silence are necessary if we are to go anywhere with it. And one of the signs of progress is that we *desire* solitude and silence. This solitude and silence must, of course, be inspired by love of God and love of man. Then it becomes the foundations of a pervasive and gentle sympathy with other people. It is easy to distinguish a deep pray-er from a narrow one. The narrow pray-er can be a very impossible person, self-righteous, judgmental, pedestrian. We must beware of this unattractive Pharisaism that seeks self in prayer, and the virtues for display, spurred on by a need for attention. Authentic prayer lifts us up out of the slough of self-enjoyment, which frequently substitutes extra penances for the ordinary duties we ought to be doing. Thus we'll find a mother neglecting her husband and children while she gets involved in "church work," or young people refusing to help at home but eager to help transform the world. We should remember the warning of Louis Bouyer on pursuing false goals: we become "nothing more than a lamp, extinguished under the bushel, asphyxiated by its own smoke."

It is not what we do that matters but the *love* we put into what we do. When Mother Teresa of Calcutta was asked, "What will you do when you are no longer Mother General?" she answered, "I am first-class in cleaning toilets and drains....If I belong to Christ and at that moment he wants me to be cleaning the toilets, or taking care of the lepers, or talking to the president of the United States, it is all the same; because I am being what God wants me to be, and doing what he wants me to do."

With true prayer, there comes *hesychia*, the perfect pacifying of body and soul. Prayer becomes more simple, a peaceful abiding in the presence of God that overflows in good works and above all in love, which is our highest activity of all. St. Jane Frances de Chantal's servants used to say, "Madame's first director made her pray only three times a day and the whole household was upset. But the Bishop of Geneva [St. Francis de Sales] makes her pray all day long and she disturbs no one."

We know we are advancing in prayer when we see the face of the suffering Christ in our neighbors, when we see how wonderful most people are, when we respect the mystery in each other, when prayer renews and revitalizes every part of our life, including the most ordinary and the least undramatic. For it is the Spirit himself praying in us with unspeakable groanings, and his fruits are charity, joy, peace, patience, kindness, goodness, faith, modesty, continency (Gal 5:22–23).

CHAPTER 6
What About Distractions?

The Abbot Pastor was consulted by one of the brothers who said, "Many distractions come to my mind and my soul is in danger because of them." The old man took him outside and said: "Lift up your arms and catch the wind." But he answered, "I cannot." And the old man said to him: "If you cannot catch the wind, neither can you stop distractions from coming into your mind."

Distractions are not only inevitable, they are indispensable. And if not deliberately planned and chosen by us, they can help our prayer by leading us to realize our total dependence on God and our inability to do anything of ourselves. We must remain faithful and do what we can to stay with God even if we feel no sensible fervor. The level headed St. Teresa of Avila wrote to a friend: "As for the distractions you experience in reciting the Divine Office, I am subject to them as you are, and I advise you to attribute them, as I do, to weakness of the head; for Our Lord well knows that when we pray to him our intention is to pray *well*."

Distractions will always be with us, distracting us. It's how we deal with them that matters. Which means facing them peacefully and without worry, knowing in faith that beyond them or even behind them is God, wanting to possess us totally and so letting us feel our weakness, our need of him. Unless we admit our sinfulness and our weaknesses—our distractions remind us of them—we cannot go anywhere. They remind us we are sinners who beg for God's mercy, knowing he will give it to us no matter what our sins are. He will give mercy but he wants us in return to remember that with our sinfulness we should not be harsh with others, no matter how evil they seem to be or how annoying.

Distractions take the joy out of prayer, but we must remember Christ's words: "No one goes to the Father but by me." His way to the Father was the way of Gethsemani, the garden and Calvary, the cross. Dom John Chapman, speaking of the two states of consolation and dryness, reminds us that to say "O God, I love you so much" is the state of consolation. To say, "My God, I love you so little" (and to believe it) is the state of dryness. He advises us to be satisfied with either state. ("We must accept with joy the state God wills for us. We must not be merely resigned to God's will, we must *will* his will.") But were we to choose, perhaps the state of dryness is better. "Aridity is fervor, and if God wants it, it is best for us. Besides, it keeps us humble." We are told in Psalm 60 (61), "Hear my cry, O God; listen to my prayer. From the end of the earth I call to you, when my heart grows faint." "When prayer is not easy," notes Cardinal Hume, "and we do it anyway, it is a proof we are trying to love God, and if we stick to it, he will hear us for he is the one who is in search of us."

Distractions are the dissonant threads woven into the texture of our prayer, generating disgust, anxiety, and conflict. But they can also be the cause of greater spiritual progress. The more we progress, the more aware we become of the contradictions within us. This increases our discontent with ourselves, our consciousness of our limitations, and our need and desire for God. "O God, come to my assistance, O Lord, make haste to help me," the desert fathers used to repeat, groaning in the midst of overwhelming distractions, trials, and temptations. St. Benedict encourages us in the last instrument of good works, "never despair of the mercy of God." "Do you want to run away from God?" asks St. Augustine. "Run *to* God." How often St. Therese fell asleep after receiving Holy Communion. "Little children are just as dear to their parents whether asleep or awake in their arms," she said, bearing out Janet Erskine Stuart's thought that "unless you become as little children" refers more to the kingdom of prayer than to anything else. If prayer is difficult and we can't pray for even a few minutes because we can't concentrate, we have simply to come into God's presence and realize it is good to be there with or without our distractions. If we *want* to love God we *do* love him. The desire for prayer is prayer, the prayer *of* desire.

Prayer is surrender to the Holy Spirit who prays in us. As distractions glide in and out of our minds, let us gently push them out by recalling a sacred word or phrase, by reading, by calling on the Lord. If our whole prayer time is spent in this sort of thing, we have done a good thing. "The more we suffer and the more we are tempted, the more we should pray," says Charles de Foucauld. Let us always bear in mind we are praying not because we love prayer but because we love God.

If the whole time of prayer is spent in wanting to pray, your prayer is well made. When the will is turned to God, distractions are not only harmless, they are a positive good, for they give rise to humility and a consciousness of our nothingness before God.

CHAPTER 7
Am I Called to Contemplation?

> The Abbot Anthony said: "Pay attention to what I tell you: Whoever you may be, always have God before your eyes."

Many Christians are afraid of the very word *contemplation* and prefer (or are advised) to stay with their own thoughts about God, hesitating to surrender their faculties to his action, mistrusting his call to contemplation. But the saints warn us we must not think that contemplation is reserved for a chosen special few. It is meant for all Christians; it is why we have been created, and it will be our occupation in heaven forever—to dwell and remain immersed in God. And as we advance in prayer, the contemplative aspect, that is, a more simplified prayer of loving attention to God and awareness of his presence, will automatically need to predominate. It is a deepening of faith, accepting God as he is, giving our mind to him, emptying it that God may fill it, an exercise in nonpossessiveness, a going beyond the *ego*, a "laying aside of thoughts." This requires discipline because we love to hang onto our thoughts and recite them endlessly to God, heaping up "empty phrases as the Gentiles do; for they think they will be heard because of their many words" (Matt 6:7). Instead, we should strive to listen to God's word, and from his word learn the answers. In our waiting to hear the word of God, we must expect the cross.

It is a necessary element in the prayer life of one who follows Christ, who being in agony, prayed all the more. The desert fathers and mothers bear witness to the spiritual battles the contemplative goes through.

The Abbess Syncletica said, "In the beginning there are a great many battles and a good deal of suffering for those who are advancing toward God and, afterwards, inexpressible joy. It is like a man who wants to light a fire; at first he is choked by the smoke and his eyes are filled with tears, but at last he gets what he wants. So it is written, 'Our God is a consuming fire'" (Heb 12:24).

Therefore we must light the divine fire in ourselves with tears and hard work. To the fifth-century monk Cassian, renunciations of the body and soul and an asceticism involving concrete, definite acts are necessary for the contemplative life to grow. St. Benedict, writing a century later, says: "If we want to abide in the dwelling of his kingdom, we shall not arrive at it except by running with good works....therefore our hearts and our bodies must be prepared to do battle under the holy obedience of his commands." And from

St. Thérèse of Lisieux we hear: "All that remains for us is to fight. When we don't have the strength, then Jesus fights for us. Together let us put the axe to the root of the tree...." "Victory does not come in a day," she adds realistically.

When we want to pray but are unable to, and feel that God is dead or at least absent, perhaps he is leading us on to contemplation, to a deeper level of awareness. When this occurs we must consider "responding to the call of the spirit within, the call to the center where God dwells, waiting to refresh, revitalize, renew," urges Father Basil Pennington. "This simple method of entering into contemplative prayer has been aptly called *centering prayer*." There are some theologians who protest at this point that centering—which purports to be contemplative prayer—is a matter of effort; whereas contemplation is always infused, a sheer gift, always an outpouring of grace, whereby God takes hold of the soul and submerges its faculties in himself without any conscious effort on the part of the soul. "Centerers" answer that contemplation can be acquired in the sense that the soul can gradually simplify its meditation, calmly emptying their minds of thoughts by a gentle, peaceful repetition of a single prayer word or phrase—all the effect of grace, of course—but also the fruit of effort. Without taking a definite side on the controversy, Louis Bouyer implies that there is an intermediate state in which the soul is still able and even needs to meditate (even with infused contemplation the soul should meditate from time to time on Christ or his passion, etc., says St. Teresa of Avila) but is already oriented by grace toward a simplification and an elevation of its prayer, tending to cause it to go beyond all meditation and any form of prayer in which the soul itself is the principal author. Though contemplation is a gift, it can be acquired in the sense that we can prepare our souls to receive it. "The reward of the search is to go on searching," says St. Gregory of Nyssa. The more you find, the more there is to find.

Followers of the movement of centering prayer attest to the healing, transforming effects of centering in their lives, its fruits, a new, deeper dimension of faith, a finding of God beyond experience that gives them peace and freedom with regard to their own feelings and relationship with God. Though several excellent books and articles on centering are available, I shall explain briefly the basic principles as a starter and answer a few of the questions often asked. (For further elucidation, the best and most comprehensive work on centering prayer is *Daily We Touch Him* by Basil Pennington, OCSO. By the same author are a number of excellent articles and books on prayer.)

The prayer of centering is based on the principle that we go to the center of our being and from there enter into God. It is focusing on a person, Christ or the Father, or the Holy Spirit, or the three persons of the Trinity. (Love always centers on the person and the presence of the loved one.) It begins with the acceptance of the real self with its limitations and with its gifts. It is a journey of love, recognizing that God is more inward to me than I am to myself, and that the more I find him, the more I forget myself. Yet the more I find myself in him, the more the contemplative part of me knows that God loves me—my existence proves that—he accepts me as I am, with my sins, failings, and weaknesses, that he supports, sustains, and saves me.

The guidelines are incredibly simple. There are two preliminaries:

1. Choose a quiet place where you will not be interrupted. Turn off your phone, and do not be within earshot of the doorbell.
2. Take up a relaxed position. For most of us, this is sitting in a comfortable chair. It is best not to kneel.

THE RULES

1. Take a minute or so to quiet down and enter in faith to God dwelling within you. Start with a simple prayer, said interiorly or aloud, such as, "Lord, lead me into your presence that I may know you" *or* "My God, may I be one with you."
2. Choose a word or phrase, (the simpler the better) that expresses for you the love of God. This may be *God, Love, Savior, Jesus, Yahweh, My Lord and my God*, etc. Let it repeat itself within you, taking its

own pace, effortlessly, with your breathing perhaps, interior, peacefully, without thought or sound.
3. Whenever you are aware of thoughts or things coming at you, gently return to the prayer word.
4. At the end, come out quietly with a prayer like the Our Father, said slowly and interiorly if you are praying alone.

How long should I center?

Twenty minutes is the recommended time, though for some people ten minutes is preferable, for others twenty-five or thirty.

Where is the best place to do centering?

Anywhere you are not apt to be interrupted. Quiet, though desirable, is not absolutely essential. But interruption—by a person, a telephone, or doorbell—is very destructive. Centering has been done successfully in an airport or bus station, which, though noisy, was without an interruption. People in nursing homes, hospitals, prisons have excellent opportunities for centering and could transform not only their own lives and environment but affect the community or mankind by their hold on God. The saints' lives are full of stories of men and women who have hit rock-bottom in pain, misery, sin, poverty, degradation, and bitterness, have turned to God—always waiting for that turn—and started a new life, finding their invisible Friend always at their side, and with him have attained a transforming, redemptive sanctity and strength not for themselves alone but for the entire world to whom salvation has been promised in Christ Jesus, whose love for us is so deep that it is impossible to understand on earth and explainable only in heaven.

Can a lot of people do centering together?

It is best not to have more than twenty people doing it together. Some experienced centerers have said that to pray with more than ten or twelve is difficult. If it is done with a group, there should be one leader who alone will say the prayer at the beginning and the Our Father at the end, both prayers slowly and quietly.

Suppose it's not meant for me?

Even if centering is not for you, it won't hurt you to try it—like a new, strange fruit—if edible, may make you feel sick if you taste it but it won't kill you.

What about distractions?

In centering prayer, there are none. You are always praying, because your intention hasn't changed. You may not be aware of God, but you are still loving him. You deal positively with distractions: When you are aware of them, return to the prayer word. If you do this one hundred times in twenty minutes—"Beautiful," exclaims Trappist Father William Meninger. "You have made one hundred beautiful acts of love of God."

Shouldn't I give up centering if I often fall asleep during it?

Sleeping is not a problem. Your intention is to pray. You want to love God, and if you want to love him, you do love him. In the *Cloud of Unknowing* we are told to thank God if in prayer we fall asleep unawares.

Isn't centering a new gimmick, imitating Transcendental Meditation?

Only its name is new. It has a long history in the Christian and monastic tradition. Evagrius defines prayer as "the laying aside of thoughts," which is the essence of centering. When the fifth-century monks complained of their struggles with their thoughts, Cassian advised them to repeat, "O God, come to my help." St. Francis of Assisi once spent the whole night saying no other words than "My God and my all," certainly suggestive of a centering tradition. Centering prayer, therefore, based on the fourteenth-century *Cloud of Unknowing*, is a renewal of the traditional prayer of the church, leading to or preparing for contemplation. "It is not an end in itself, but a beginning," explains Thomas Keating, OCSO, "not to be done for the sake of an experience but for the sake of its fruits in one's life."

Centering prayer is a discipline, a commitment to the unknown, a game of love. In it you have to face the boredom within you, especially if you lead a very active life, because achievement here is subordinated to love. You do not achieve, you receive. (It has been found that high-powered businessmen and women do not relish centering. They are too achievement oriented. They can be loving, generous, and giving but they cannot receive.) Centering is a matter of receiving. The less we do, the more God does.

If the centering is authentic, fidelity in the duties of life will go on. Charity will take over more and more. You will feel a unity with everyone and with all being, in that unity with Christ and with all that is. You will learn to love your loved ones in a new way, the way God loves them, not in a dependent or dominating way. Your sufferings will be redemptive. You will relate to God as not-God, feeling his absence, feeling a sense of the loss of values because of a loss of faith, the day-to-day agony of our times. You will share in the agony of our time, and because you will be drawn into the redemptive work of the mystical Body of Christ, you will see the purpose and meaning of life as daily you live the life, the passion, death, and resurrection of the Lord.

CHAPTER 8
Mary

> The Abbot Isaac said: "I was sitting with the Abbot Poemen one day and I saw him in ecstasy. As I knew him very well I begged him to tell me about it. He answered, 'My thought was with Holy Mary the Mother of God, as she wept by the Cross of the Savior. I wish I could always weep like that.'"

No book on Christian prayer would be complete without a mention of Mary, who has such a special place in our prayer. She is the ideal of perfect response to God, of listening and waiting for the word of God. In the last specific mention of her in the Bible, we read that she was continuing "steadfastly in prayer" with the women and the apostles and disciples, both men and women, (Acts 1) after the resurrection of Christ and just before the descent of the Holy Spirit.

The pray-er *par excellence*, she teaches us why and when and how we should pray to the Lord: "Do whatever he tells you" (John 2:5). Often she "understood not" what was being done to her, but she let herself be led by the Spirit, keeping all things "carefully in her heart." Her Magnificat is the embodiment of all prayer: the fruit of her reading and meditating on the words of the Old Testament and the summation of praise and contemplation.

We see in Mary the one perfect exemplar of the Christian life. In her alone is found the fullness of Christ's gifts to the Mystical Body. But she is not just an example for us; she introduces us into the mystery of Christ not so much by her example as by her being. Her sanctity is the outcome of her divine maternity; so, too, is her power. St. Bernard teaches that God willed us to have nothing that did not pass through the hands of Mary. Through her God came to us and she continues to be the purest reservoir and channel of his graces. Her role is to receive and to give Christ. "What she was at the start, we hope to become at the end," says Thomas Keating, "that is, immaculate and transparent."

"Mary taught men a new way of praying," says Adrienne von Speyr. "In prayer she is a thing in the hands of her Son; she not only allows herself to be led but administered, so to say, handed out to all. And the fruit of her gift comes to light in the Son's words: 'He who does the will of my Father is my mother.' Only someone who misunderstood those words could regard them as a rebuke, for in fact they are the fulfillment of her offer. She remained silent, accepting the words as the most perfect the Lord could say to her; she kept silence so that others might hear them better. She understood that he was disposing of her assent and her life."

Mary spoke few words. Flooded with grace, she stayed silent in adoration of her Son. She contemplated the mystery of the Incarnation wrought in and through her, and she continually praised and thanked God who had chosen her, returning all glory to him. She knew no will of her own but that of perfect conformity to the will of God. "Be it done to me according to your word" is always the answer of this perfect hearer and perfect doer of the word of God. How hard it must have been for her to see the Christ child rejected even before birth (there was no room at the inn) and born in a stable. Mary knows well how to comfort the afflicted, the poor, the rejected!

In her, matter reaches its supreme glorification from the beginning—immaculately conceived, to the end—assumed into heaven, body and soul. "With a full heart and impeded by no sin, she devoted herself totally as a handmaid of the Lord to the person and work of her Son" (*Lumen Gentium* 56). Her concern was not for herself but for God—"Be it done unto me according to your word," and for her neighbor—"They have no wine." If we do not learn from Mary to love our neighbor more, something is wrong with our devotion or we do not love her very much. Never did she think of herself, but of others and their needs: her son, her kinswoman, Elizabeth, Simeon and Anna, the elders in the temple, her friends at the marriage feast of Cana, the disciples in the Upper Room.

Father Perrin points out that it would be false to think that we must necessarily go to Jesus through Mary. It is also true that others reach Mary through Jesus. After meditating on Christ's life and words, they sometimes come very late to an understanding of what Mary has been to Christ and what she must become for them. But if Mary has no part in our lives, it is very tragic indeed. She who was utterly sinless, "our tainted nature's solitary boast" (Wordsworth), loved God as no other creature loved him, and she loves *us* as no other created being loves us: We were given to her by her son in that supreme hour of our redemption when he was dying on the cross. And from that hour, she has taken us to her own.

green press
INITIATIVE

Paulist Press is committed to preserving ancient forests and natural resources. We elected to print this title on 30% post consumer recycled paper, processed chlorine free. As a result, for this printing, we have saved:

> 1 Tree (40' tall and 6-8" diameter)
> 1 Million BTUs of Total Energy
> 129 Pounds of Greenhouse Gases
> 581 Gallons of Wastewater
> 37 Pounds of Solid Waste

Paulist Press made this paper choice because our printer, Thomson-Shore, Inc., is a member of Green Press Initiative, a nonprofit program dedicated to supporting authors, publishers, and suppliers in their efforts to reduce their use of fiber obtained from endangered forests.

For more information, visit www.greenpressinitiative.org

Environmental impact estimates were made using the Environmental Defense Paper Calculator. For more information visit: www.papercalculator.org.